GARMADON'S BAD GUY TRAINING MANUAL

Scholastic Inc.

ISBN: 978-1-338-64164-6

10 9 8 7 6 5 4 3 2 1   20 21 22 23 24

Printed in China   95
First edition 2020

Book design by Cheung Tai

Welcome, Villains!

What does it take to be a masterful villain? You will need more than a scary costume and a catchy slogan. To be a truly great villain, you need a clever mind, a desire to rule the world—and practice! Lots of practice. In this training guide, you'll find everything you need to be as bad as the baddest baddie around. If you're not on Ninjago's Most Wanted List by the end of this book, then my name isn't Garmadon!

First, it's time to learn something from some already famous villains.

Baddest Deeds:

- Stole the Golden Weapons
- Released the evil Overlord

My younger brother, Wu, thinks that the day I was bitten by the Great Devourer was a terrible one. Ha! He is only jealous because the bite from that snake left me with great power . . . more power than Wu could ever dream of.

But that bite only made me stronger than I am. For I am the descendant of the Oni, an ancient race of evil beings. From the Oni, I received my element: Destruction. Even without the snake poison in my veins, I am a force to be reckoned with. No one—not even my son, Lloyd— can stop me!

Baddest Deeds:

- Kidnapping Nya and bringing her to the Underworld
- Attacking Jay's parents

Samukai is ruthless, cruel—and overconfident. He thought he could battle me and win, but I defeated him (with some help from my brother, Wu), and banished him to the Underworld. There, he became king of the Skulkin—until I showed up, took over as ruler, and made him my lieutenant.

Always treacherous, Samukai tried to take the four Golden Weapons for himself. But their power destroyed him and he ended up in the Departed Realm. Later, his spirit escaped from there and he tangled with the Ninja—and lost.

Skull Motorbike!

Samukai's army of Skulkin soldiers have nothing to lose. They don't need to eat or sleep. They can pull apart their bones and put themselves back together again. They're a little hard to control, but if I ever need them again I know where to look—in the Underworld.

PYTHOR P. CHUMSWORTH

Baddest Deeds:

- Unleashing the Great Devourer on Ninjago
- Helping the Digital Overlord seek revenge on the Ninja

Pythor was never the most powerful of the Serpentine, but he might be the cleverest. He survived the Serpentine Wars and united the snake tribes to release the Great Devourer on Ninjago.

Things didn't work out so great for him, though. He got devoured by the Devourer. He managed to survive, only to be turned into a tiny terror thanks to a shrinking pill. He is back to being a full-sized serpent, but his whereabouts are unknown. I've got to give it to him: he knows how to save his own skin!

Anacondrai

Hypnobrai

Fangpyre

Constrictai

Venomari

Baddest Deeds:

- He is the source of all Darkness.

- As the Golden Master, he wanted to enslave every living creature on Ninjago.

This ancient deity first battled with my father, the First Spinjitzu Master. Years later, he asked me to join forces with him, and I agreed. Some say I was foolish to do so, because he possessed my body and we transformed into a giant dragon. But I will never forget the power I felt that day!

The Ninja thought they defeated the Overlord, but he came back as a digital virus, and then the Golden Master, the most powerful being ever created. The Ninja Zane sacrificed himself to defeat him, but the Overlord's spirit can never die. Maybe one day we will join forces again!

During his battle with my father, the Overlord created the Stone Army. These indestructible warriors did anything he commanded, without question. Sometimes I wish I had minions like this. So many of mine have been real blockheads!

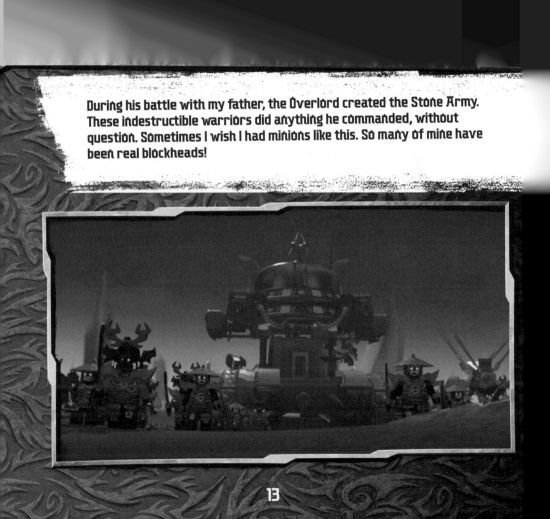

Baddest Deeds:

- They captured Master Wu so he could be turned into a cyborg.
- They traveled to space to retrieve the Golden Weapons for the Digital Overlord.

These villains are kind of like the Ninjas, but without souls—or annoying wisecracks! They are advanced combat robots designed for battle by tech genius Cyrus Borg, after he became possessed by the Digital Overlord.

Their main weakness is that they can be reprogrammed. When that happens, they end up like that do-gooder Ninja, Zane. I think any villain who can change sides so easily isn't a true villain at all!

General Cryptor was the commander of the Nindroids. During the Golden Master's assault in Ninjago City, Cryptor was shattered in battle. He returned when his spirit escaped the Departed Realm, but he was sent back when he accidentally hit himself with his own weapon. Not his finest moment!

He's shorter than the other Nindroids, because the factory ran out of metal. But this tiny terror is sneaky and skilled, proving that size doesn't matter if you want to be a villain!

Baddest Deeds:

- Masterminding the Serpentine War
- Stealing the elements from the Elemental Masters

Some people say that Chen is a better villain than I am, because he trained me, and I say that those people are wrong. But I have to give Chen some credit. He may not have been born with any Elemental powers, but his brilliant mind makes up for that.

Chen figured out how to trick all of the Elemental Masters into competing in a Tournament of Elements. He managed to steal their powers and transform himself into an Anacondrai. He finally got the power he wanted, even though he ended up banished in the Departed Realm.

THE MANY FACES OF MASTER CHEN . . .

The master who taught his pupils to win, no matter what the cost.

The beloved owner of Ninjago's most popular noodle shop.

The confident ringmaster of the Tournament of Elements.

In his Anacondrai form, achieving the power he had always dreamed of having.

Baddest Deeds:

- Master Chen's daughter served as his spy during the Tournament of Elements.

I almost didn't include Skylor in this guide, because she betrayed her father so that she could help the Ninja. But her remarkable Elemental power is worth studying.

Skylor is the Elemental Master of Amber, the power of absorption. This means that she can copy the power of another Elemental Master. A skilled fighter, she could have taken down the Ninja if she hadn't had such a soft heart!

All Skylor has to do is touch another Elemental Master to absorb their power.

Once she absorbs the power, she can turn that Elemental energy into powerful attacks.

Skylor can absorb more than one Element at a time, but that can quickly drain her energy.

Baddest Deeds:

- Casting dark magic spells against the Ninja
- Opening up the Cursed Realm

Clouse and I both trained under Master Chen, who gave me the title of Lord Garmadon and not Clouse. Ever since then, he has burned with the fire of revenge.

Bitter and angry, Clouse grew a creepy mustache and turned to dark magic. He battles with spells and the help of his giant purple serpent. I think his dark powers might be what saved him when he survived the destruction of the Cursed Realm. They are pretty impressive, but he will never be as impressive as I am!

CLOUSE WAS MASTER CHEN'S RIGHT-HAND MAN, BUT THERE WERE OTHERS WHO SERVED CHEN SO THEY COULD BE TURNED INTO ANACONDRAI. EACH DISCIPLE WAS MARKED WITH A UNIQUE ANACONDRAI TATTOO ON HIS OR HER BACK.

Eyezor:
He only has one eye, but he's twice as tough as any of Chen's minions.

Zugu:
This former sumo wrestler is a mountain of muscle.

Kapau and Chope:
If you're not making it as a villain, do what these bumbling bozos did and change your name to something cool. That's how they moved up in the ranks.

Baddest Deeds:

- Possessed the body of the Green Ninja, Lloyd
- Released the Preeminent from the Cursed Realm

Ah, Morro. He's one of my favorite villains because he was created by my brother, Wu! That's right. He was a pupil of Wu's, who filled his head with dreams of becoming the Green Ninja. When he wasn't chosen, he left Wu and lost his life in the Caves of Despair.

That's when he became a ghost. He escaped from the Cursed Realm and freed the Ghost Warriors. When they released the monstrous spirit of the Cursed Realm, the Preeminent, they came closer to destroying the realm of Ninjago—than anyone but me.

MORRO'S GHOST WARRIORS WERE SOME OF THE FIERCEST FOES THE NINJA HAD EVER FACED!

When Bow Master Soul Archer's arrow hits you, you will become a ghost!

Blade Master Bansha can meld with your mind and take over your body.

He might be a ghost, but Scythe Master Ghoultar has a big appetite for puffy pot stickers.

Baddest Deeds:

- Terrorized Ninjago City in his pirate ship

- Imprisoned the Sky Pirate captain, Nadakhan, in the Teapot of Tyrahn

Captain Soto likes to brag and say that he defeated me, Lloyd Garmadon, in battle. That may be technically true, but it's not the whole story.

Soto was the original captain of the Destiny's Bounty. He and his crew perished after No-Eyed Pete steered the ship into a rock. Two hundred years later, I accidentally resurrected them. Weakened by the use of the Golden Weapons, I found myself locked up by Soto and his pirates. But if it weren't for me, he couldn't have locked me up in the first place!

ACRONIX AND KRUX

Baddest Deeds:

- Built a time-traveling weapon, the Iron Doom
- Created an army of Vermillion snake warriors that almost destroyed Ninjago

If you've got a minute, I'll tell you the story of these twin brothers, the Elemental Masters of Time. I have to warn you, it's quite alarming.

Aargh! What is it about Acronix and Krux that makes me want to use time puns? Anyway, these Time Twins began their life of crime years ago, when they betrayed the Elemental Masters. After years of being separated, they built a time machine and tried to get their revenge. I have to admit, I like the way they think! It's too bad their plan didn't work.

ARE THEY HUMAN? ARE THEY SNAKE? THEY'RE BOTH! MEET THE VERMILLION WARRIORS, DIRECT DESCENDANTS OF THE GREAT DEVOURER WHO DID THE BIDDING OF ACRONIX AND KRUX.

Commander Blunck loves nothing more than a *tassssty ssssssnack*!

Supreme Commander Machia's hair is a clue to her snaky nature.

Along with Machia and Blunck, Commander Raggmunk can command the Vermillion warriors with the combined power of their minds.

Baddest Deeds:

- Brought Lord Garmadon back from the Departed Realm
- Ruled Ninjago City alongside Garmadon and led the fight against the Resistance

Some called her the Jade Princess of Ninjago. Others knew her as the mysterious Quiet One, the leader of the Sons of Garmadon biker gang. To me, she was like a daughter.

Like the best villains, Harumi's heart hardened when she was a child. She lost her parents to the Great Devourer and vowed revenge on the Ninja who didn't protect the city. Her diabolical plan forced the cowering Ninja into the shadows. For that, she will always have a special place in my black heart.

HARUMI KNEW THAT TO FORM AN ARMY TO FIGHT THE NINJA, SHE'D HAVE TO REACH OUT TO MEMBERS OF SOCIETY WHO DIDN'T FOLLOW THE RULES. SHE RECRUITED BIKERS TO FORM THE SONS OF GARMADON. SHE EQUIPPED THEM WITH STOLEN ONI MASKS TO GIVE THEM SPECIAL ABILITIES.

Killow terrorizes the streets of Ninjago on his Oni Chopper. Wearing the Oni Mask of Deception, he could move objects just by thinking of it.

Loud and angry UltraViolet always knew how to keep the Sons of Garmadon in line. Wearing the Oni Mask of Hatred turned her body into stone, making her unstoppable!

Baddest Deeds:

- Captured the Ninja after they crash-landed in the Realm of Oni and Dragons
- Ordered his Dragon Hunters to stalk and enslave dragons
- Forced prisoners to fight dragons in a deadly arena known as The Pit

While Harumi spent her life seeking revenge against the Ninja, Iron Baron sought revenge against a dragon: Firstbourne. The first dragon ever created, she claimed an arm and a leg of the Baron's during a fierce battle.

In his quest for revenge, Iron Baron formed the Dragon Hunters from outcasts of this dangerous realm. I must admit, I admire his leadership style. Iron Baron ruled his Dragon Hunters through fear, lies, and deception. It works every time!

LIFE ISN'T EASY IN THE REALM OF ONI AND DRAGONS. THE HOT SUN BEATS DOWN EVERY DAY, AND LITTLE GROWS IN THE RED SAND. THE IRON BARON PROMISED HIS DRAGON HUNTERS THAT IN ORDER TO SURVIVE, THEY NEEDED TO STICK WITH HIM.

The Dragon Hunters' weapons are made of vengestone, a mysterious substance that can drain the elemental powers from a dragon—or an Elemental Master.

Heavy Metal was Iron Baron's second-in command. She ended up betraying him by helping the Ninja.

Baddest Deeds:

- Almost succeeded in wiping out all Creation

He called himself the Bringer of Doom. He tried to engulf all of Ninjago in Destruction and wipe out Creation. I have to admit, I admire a villain who thinks big!

The Omega Oni is the leader of the Oni—a race of demonic beings who embody pure evil. With his staff, the Omega can summon leagues of Oni warriors to fight for him. His dark energy manifests as tentacles that can trap his opponents. But with all that power, he has one major weakness: Creation.

FOR CENTURIES THE DEMONIC ONI, KNOWN AS THE BRINGERS OF DOOM, STAYED IN THE REALM OF ONI AND DRAGON. LED BY THE OMEGA, THEY ESCAPED THROUGH THE REALM CRYSTAL INTO NINJAGO CITY. THEIR CLOUD OF DARKNESS PETRIFIES ANYONE IT TOUCHES. ONLY THE ELEMENT OF GOLDEN POWER CAN DEFEAT THE ONI DARKNESS.

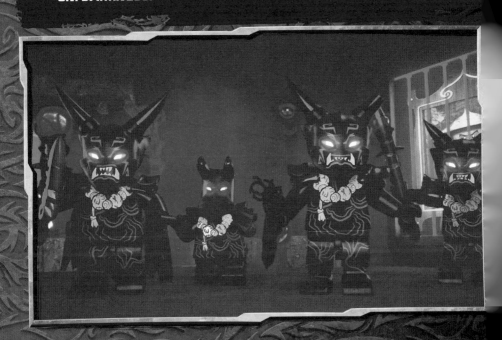

Baddest Deeds:

- Stole the Element of Fire from Kai
- Attacked Ninjago City
- Banished Zane to the Never Realm

I don't laugh very much. But when I do, it's when my brother, Wu, creates a villain. That's what happened years ago, when Wu betrayed his friendship with Aspheera. But first, he taught her the art of Spinjitzu, making her the most powerful Serpentine who has ever lived.

After spending ages trapped in a pyramid, the Ninja accidentally freed her. (That made me laugh, too!) With the help of her Pyro Vipers, she attacked Ninjago City in her quest to banish Wu to the Never Realm. She sent Zane to this land of eternal winter instead, breaking Wu's heart and getting rid of one of the Ninja at the same time. Now that's what I call a happy ending!

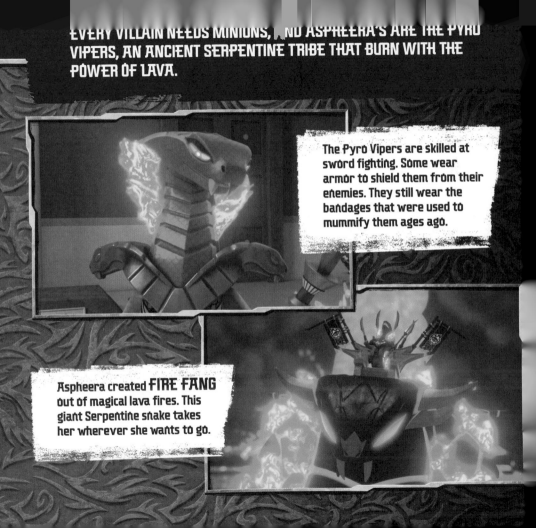

EVERY VILLAIN NEEDS MINIONS, AND ASPHEERA'S ARE THE PYRO VIPERS, AN ANCIENT SERPENTINE TRIBE THAT BURN WITH THE POWER OF LAVA.

The Pyro Vipers are skilled at sword fighting. Some wear armor to shield them from their enemies. They still wear the bandages that were used to mummify them ages ago.

Aspheera created **FIRE FANG** out of magical lava fires. This giant Serpentine snake takes her wherever she wants to go.

Baddest Deeds:

- Capturing players inside the Prime Empire video game
- Plotting to unleash evil game creatures on Ninjago

Plenty of the villains in this guide are undead, but Unagami is the first one who has never technically been alive. (Even the Digital Overlord once had a physical form.) Unagami is an artificial intelligence, and ruler of Prime Empire—a sprawling digital game world.

Abandoned by his creator, Unagami has been luring players into the game and stealing their energy. With that energy, Unagami hopes to build a portal into Ninjago City to finally confront his father.

I think that Unagami has the potential to be an impressive force of destruction. But while he may be artificial, his emotions are real—and in the end, they could be his downfall.

The Red Visors might be primitive and mindless, but they're dangerous. Armed with laser blades, blasters, and jetpacks, they can travel rapidly through the game. And when they catch you, they'll convert you into an energy cube!

Unagami's drones broadcast their video feeds directly to their master—as well as pick up the energy cubes.

SINISTER SETTINGS

NOW THAT YOU'VE MET THE OTHER VILLAINS, IT'S TIME TO TAKE A TOUR OF SOME IMPORTANT LOCATIONS. THESE ARE ALL PLACES WHERE YOU WON'T USUALLY FIND NINJA—UNLESS THEY'RE LOOKING FOR TROUBLE!

THE UNDERWORLD

This is the home of the Skulkin, the skeletons of warriors who received new life thanks to the strange powers of this dark realm. Samukai ruled here for a long time until Lord Garmadon found himself there.

If you want to explore the Underworld without making the ultimate sacrifice, there is a portal in the ancient Fire Temple that will take you there.

THE CURSED REALM

Like the Underworld, the Cursed Realm is one of the Sixteen Realms. It's also the darkest, gloomiest, and scariest place to ever exist. It was meant as a home for cursed souls, but the living could travel there through a portal—although very few have dared to do that.

The Cursed Realm was linked with its ruler, the terrifying embodiment of evil known as the Preeminent. Some believe that when the Preeminent was destroyed, the Cursed Realm was lost forever.

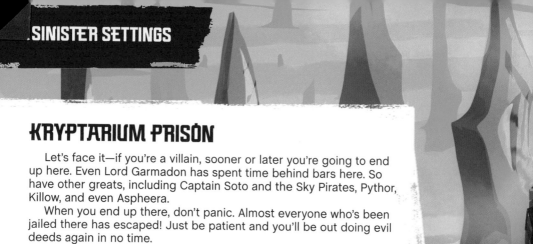

KRYPTARIUM PRISON

Let's face it—if you're a villain, sooner or later you're going to end up here. Even Lord Garmadon has spent time behind bars here. So have other greats, including Captain Soto and the Sky Pirates, Pythor, Killow, and even Aspheera.

When you end up there, don't panic. Almost everyone who's been jailed there has escaped! Just be patient and you'll be out doing evil deeds again in no time.

THE LOST CITY OF OUROBOROS

Also known as the Forsaken City (which is a lot easier to spell!), Ouroboros is the lost city of the Serpentine. It was buried underneath the Sea of Sand after the Serpentine War.

More than buildings were buried in Ouroboros. For many years, the enormous serpent known as the Great Devourer was trapped here. There has been little action here since the Great Devourer was released, so it should be a safe place now. But in the world of Ninjago, you never know . . .

THE REALM OF ONI AND DRAGONS

A vast wasteland of hot sand and brutal sunlight, you might think this would be the perfect location for your villain's hideout. (The Iron Baron thought so, and it didn't work out for him.) This was the first realm ever created, and for a very long time only two beings lived there: the demonic Oni, masters of Destruction, and the Dragons, the masters of Creation.

These days there are no Oni living there, and the Dragons are guarded by Faith and Firstbourne. So while it may be a tempting to build your hideout there, you'll have to get through Faith first—and that won't be easy.

THE NEVER REALM

Once a peaceful (but cold) land of eternal winter, the Never Realm changed the day Zane, the Ninja of Ice, was banished there by Aspheera. He was found by General Vex, who wiped him of his memories and convinced him to use his powers to take over the realm.

Zane became a cold, cruel Ice Emperor manipulated by Vex. With his army of Blizzard Samurai, they terrorized the inhabitants of this realm. It was a villain's paradise, until those annoying Ninja showed up.

ENEMY NINJA: Lloyd

ALSO KNOWN AS: The Green Ninja

ELEMENT: Master of Power

WEAPON OF CHOICE: Sword

STRENGTHS AND POWERS:

- Spinjitzu
- As the Green Ninja, Lloyd topples his opponents with powerful energy blasts.
- Because he is the grandson of the First Spinjitsu Master, he has both Oni and Dragon blood running through his veins.
- Lloyd is the only Ninja who can wield the Golden Power.

WEAKNESSES:

- Lloyd has no ambition! He could have used the Golden Power to do anything, but he split it up between the Ninja instead.
- He takes everything Master Wu says very seriously.

NOTES:

- Lloyd led the Resistance when Lord Garmadon and Harumi took over Ninjago City.

ENEMY NiNJA: Kai

ALSO KNOWN AS: The Ninja of Fire

ELEMENT: Master of Fire

WEAPON OF CHOICE: Sword or Katana

STRENGTHS AND POWERS:

- Spinjitzu
- Can blast his enemies with powerful flames and fireballs.

WEAKNESSES:

- His hot temper can make him act without thinking.
- Kai will do anything to protect his sister.
- He has a fear of water.

NOTES:

- Kai almost lost faith in himself when he lost his powers to Aspheera. But it looks like they're coming back. Drat!

ENEMY NINJA: Nya

ALSO KNOWN AS: The Ninja of Water

ELEMENT: Master of Water

WEAPON OF CHOICE: Spear

STRENGTHS AND POWERS:
- Spinjitzu
- Nya creates powerful water attacks.
- She is an excellent builder and technician.

WEAKNESSES:
- Her water powers don't work well in freezing temperatures.
- As the last Ninja to master her element, she is still learning about her powers.

NOTES:
- Nya was the original Mech warrior known as Samurai X.

ENEMY NINJA: Cole

ALSO KNOWN AS: The Ninja of Earth

ELEMENT: Master of Earth

WEAPON OF CHOICE: Scythe or Hammer

STRENGTHS AND POWERS:
- Spinjitzu
- Cole can create earthquakes just by jumping on the ground.
- He can toss around boulders as casually as baseballs.
- With his Earth Punch, he can use his arms like battering rams.

WEAKNESSES:
- Cake. Cookies. Noodles. Dumplings . . .
- He is very protective of his teammates, which sometimes leaves him vulnerable.

NOTES:
- Cole's grandfather was the former Master of Earth.

ENEMY NINJA: Jay

ALSO KNOWN AS: The Ninja of Lightning

ELEMENT: Master of Lightning

WEAPON OF CHOICE: Nunchuks

STRENGTHS AND POWERS:
- Spinjitzu
- Jay is a great inventor.
- He moves with lightning speed.
- His Lightning Punch wallops his opponents with an electric charge.

WEAKNESSES:
- Jay loses his cool when people he loves are in danger.
- He tells the worst jokes!

NOTES:
- Jay's parents are Ed and Edna Walker, inventors and owners of a junkyard. But his birth father is famous actor Cliff Gordon, and his birth mother was the former Elemental Master of Lightning.

ENEMY NINJA: Zane

ALSO KNOWN AS: The Titanium Ninja

ELEMENT: Master of Ice

WEAPON OF CHOICE: Shurikens

STRENGTHS AND POWERS:
- Spinjitzu
- In battle, he keeps his cool when the action heats up.
- He's a great problem solver.
- He can shoot Shurikens from his wrists.

WEAKNESSES:
- Zane can be rebooted, or have his memory wiped clean. That is how General Vex turned him into the Ice Emperor.
- He has shown more than once that he is willing to sacrifice himself for others. That goes against everything villains stand for!

NOTES:
- Zane wasn't always the Titanium Ninja. After the Digital Overlord destroyed him, he rebuilt himself to become a stronger, better Nindroid.

ENEMY NiNJA: Master Wu

ALSO KNOWN AS: Son of the First Spinjitzu Master

ELEMENT: Master of Creation

WEAPON OF CHOiCE: Staff

POWERS AND STRENGTHS:

- His Oni blood has granted him a long life. He is over one thousand years old.
- Few opponents can stand against his powerful Spinjitzu tornado, which holds the combined power of all four elements.
- Wu is skilled in combat.
- He can summon an Elemental Creation Dragon.

WEAKNESSES:

- He puts the needs of other people before his own. What's the point of that?
- As a younger man, his curiosity often got him into trouble.

NOTES:

- Thanks to the Reversal Blade, Wu once turned into a baby and was kidnapped by the Sons of Garmadon. He re-aged quickly and is now a bearded old man once again.

DARETH

He calls himself the Brown Ninja, but the only power this bumbling do-gooder has is to embarrass himself!

MISAKO

She is the mother of Lloyd Garmadon, the Green Ninja, and a skill fighter with a Katana.

CLUTCH POWERS

The Ninja seem to admire this adventurer, but the only thing this explorer seems able to find is trouble!

LIL' NELSON AND ANTÓNIA

Don't let the innocent faces of these newspaper-selling kids fool you. They're wannabee Ninja and if you run into them, they'll be nothing but trouble!

Do you have what it takes to join us in our quest to eliminate the Ninja once and for all?

WE WILL SSSSEEEEE HOW SSSSSSMART YOU ARE!

WHO ARE YOU, ANYWAY?

If you're going to be a villain, you're going to have to have a cool name. Choose your own, or use this formula to generate one.

CHOOSE ONE BASED ON YOUR BIRTHDAY

JANUARY: Frozen

FEBRUARY: Doctor

MARCH: Savage

APRIL: Commander

MAY: The Great

JUNE: Wicked

JULY: Vicious

AUGUST: Creepy

SEPTEMBER: Crooked

OCTOBER: Count

NOVEMBER: Master

DECEMBER: General

CHOOSE ONE BASED ON YOUR FAVORITE COLOR

WHITE = Specter

BLACK = Banshee

RED = Monster

ORANGE = Shocker

GREEN = Evil

BLUE = Behemoth

PURPLE = Barbarian

SILVER = Beast

GOLD = Fiend

PINK = Mayhem

TURQUOISE = Chaos

Write your villain name here:

_____

Now, draw your villain costume:

VILLAIN QUESTIONNAIRE

What quality do you have that would make you a great villain?

Kungfu , Speed , hideing

What is your evil superpower?

invisadilaty

What is your biggest weakness?

If you could join forces with any Ninjago villain, who would it be?

What kind of villainous vehicle do you want Killow to build for you?

Moterbike

Where will your hidden headquarters be?

jungle

INTERCEPTED!

The Nindroids have intercepted a message that Master Wu sent to the Ninja, but their circuits scrambled it. Rearrange the letters in each word to figure out what the Ninja are up to.

J A N N I !   T E G   C K B A   O T

_ _ _ _ _ _   _ _ _   _ _ _ _   _ _

H E T   O A T R M N S E Y   W O N !

_ _ _   _ _ _ _ _ _ _ _ _   _ _ _ _ !

O Y U   N E D E   O T   C A N E L

_ _ _   _ _ _ _   _ _   _ _ _ _ _

O U Y R   O O M R S !

_ _ _ _   _ _ _ _ _ !

T I   S K O O L   I K L E   A

_ _   _ _ _ _ _   _ _ _ _   _

O O R N T D A   T I H   M E H T !

_ _ _ _ _ _ _   _ _ _   _ _ _ _ !

69

NINJA QUIZ

How well do you know your enemy, the Ninja? Take this quiz to prove that you know the basic facts about them.

1. Which Ninja took dance lessons as a kid?

a. Jay ✗
b. Nya ✗
c. Cole ✓
d. Kai ✗

2. Which Ninja used to be Samurai X?

a. Lloyd ✗
b. Cole ✗
c. Kai ✗
d. Nya ✓

3. **Which Ninja got expelled from Darkley's Boarding School for Bad Boys?**

   a. Kai ✗
   b. Cole ✗
   c. Jay ✗
   d. Lloyd ✓

4. **What is the name of Zane's original creator?**

   a. Ed Walker ✗
   b. Dr. Julien ✗
   c. Cyrus Borg ✗
   d. The Iron Baron ✓

5. **What do Jay's parents, Ed and Edna, do for a living?**

   a. They run a junkyard. ✗

   b. They are standup comedians. ✓

   c. They run a noodle shop. ✗

   d. They are scientists. ✗

6. **Which Ninja lived as a ghost for a while?**

   a. Cole ✓

   b. Jay ✗

   c. Nya ✗

   d. Kai ✗

7. **What is Master Wu's favorite beverage?**

   a. Milk ✗

   b. Energy drink ✗

   c. Tea ✓

   d. Water ✗

8. Which Ninja has a connection to the former villain, Skylor?

a. Nya ✗
b. Jay ✗
c. Cole ✗
d. Kai ✓

VILLAINOUS VEHICLES

Every villain needs a set of wicked wheels. Take inspiration from these, and then design your own!

Iron Baron's armored Dieselnaut has wheels and treads tough enough for the rough terrain of the Realm of Oni and Dragons. It's loaded with weapons for capturing dragons or ninja.

Maybe you want something more classic, like a Skulkin's Skull Motorbike that's built for speed.

Killow added some sinister accessories to his chopper, like the spinning saw blade by the front wheel.

WHAT WILL YOUR VEHICLE LOOK LIKE?

LAUGH BREAK

Even villains laugh once in a while. It's even better if you can develop an evil laugh. You know, like a cackle, or a "mwah-ha-ha!" Go ahead, try out your evil laugh! Now that you're in a funny mood, fill in the speech bubbles in these scenes. Seeing the Ninja in trouble always cheers me up!

BATTLE IN THE HIDEOUT!

Killow is guarding the SOG hideout when he hears the roar of engines outside. The door busts open and Lloyd, Zane, and Nya race inside.

What happens next?

(Finish the story on the blank lines below.)

_____

_____

_____

_____

_____

_____

_____

_____

_____

_____

_____

_____

_____

_____

_____

_____

_____

SERPENTINE SEARCH

There is always a secret to opening the tomb of a Serpentine tribe. What is one way to open it? To find out, search for these words beginning with the letter "S" in this puzzle and circle them. The letters you didn't circle will spell out what you need to do.

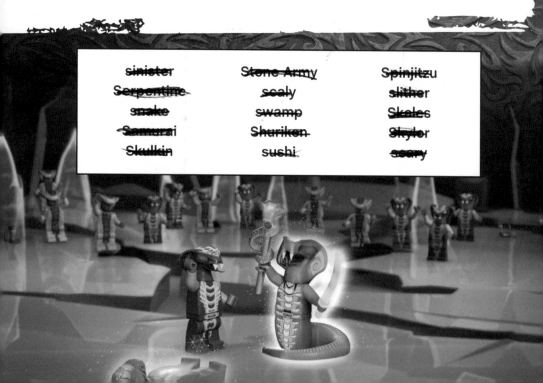

sinister ~~sinister~~

~~Serpentine~~

~~snake~~

~~Samurai~~

~~Skulkin~~

~~Stone Army~~

~~scaly~~

swamp

~~Shuriken~~

sushi

~~Spinjitzu~~

~~slither~~

~~Skales~~

~~Skylor~~

~~scary~~

How can you open the Serpentine tomb?

First, search for all the words beginning with the letter "s" in this puzzle and circle them. Don't forget to look for words spelled backwards! The letters you didn't circle will spell out what you need to do. There is one word already filled out

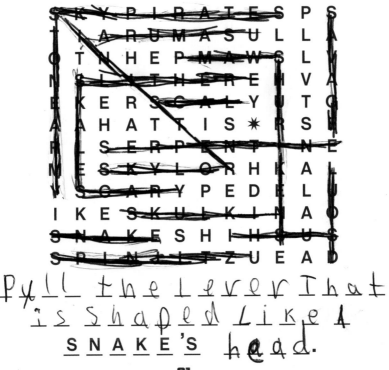

Pull the lever that is shaped like a **S N A K E**'s head.

DECODE JAY'S DIARY

One of Unagamai's Red Visors has stolen a page from the diary of Jay, the Ninja of Lightning, but it's in code! What shocking secret does it hold? Use the key on the next page to crack the code.

CODE:

A	B	C	D	E	F	G	H	I	J	K	L	M	N	O	P	Q	R	S	T	U	V	W	X	Y	Z
Z	Y	X	W	V	U	T	S	R	Q	P	O	N	M	L	K	J	I	H	G	F	E	D	C	B	A

DSB ZIV XZGH HL TLLW
ZG ERWVL TZNVH?

YVXZFHV GSVB SZEV
MRMV OREVH!

_ _ _   _ _ _   _ _ _ _

_ _   _ _ _ _ _   _ _ _ _ _ ?

_ _ _ _ _ _ _   _ _ _ _   _ _ _ _

_ _ _ _   _ _ _ _ _ !

MINION MATCH

Every villain needs minions! Match the minion on the left page to the villain on the right page.

Write the letter of each minion to the villain he, she, or it works for.

1. MASTER CHEN _____

2. HARUMI _____

3. MORRO _____

4. SAMUKAI _____

PYRAMID PUZZLE

Complete the pyramid. The number in each block should be the total of the two numbers below it.

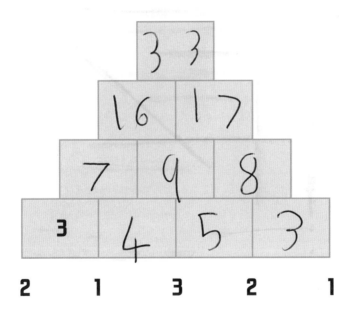

33

16   17

7   9   8

3   4   5   3

2   1   3   2   1

1. I am the Ghost,
   Who will scare you the _____!

2. I'm brave and I'm bold,
   And I'll steal all of your _____!

3. The Underworld's the best!
   The dead there get no _____!

4. My army can't be beat!
   They burn with lava _____!

Now come up with your rhyming catchphrase!

_____

_____

_____

_____

_____

CAN YOU REACH LEVEL THIRTEEN?

Here's your final test: The Ninja are trapped in Level Thirteen of the Prime Empire video game. Solve each of these riddles correctly to reach them. If you're stuck, unscramble the answers.

LEVEL 1: What has hands but can't clap? *a lkocc*

LEVEL 2: What do you have to break before you can use it? *na geg*

LEVEL 3: What goes up but never comes down? *rouy gea*

LEVEL 4: What starts with T, ends with T, and has tea in it? *ottpea*

LEVEL 5: What gets wetter and wetter the more it dries? *a wolet*

LEVEL 6: What is something you will never see again? *yyatsrdee*

LEVEL 7: What is the Iron Baron's favorite kind of music? *vhaey lteam*

_____

LEVEL 8: What is easy to get into and difficult to get out of? *boulert*

_____

LEVEL 9: What is full of holes but still holds water? *a gnopes*

_____

LEVEL 10: What gets bigger, the more you take away from it? *a leho*

_____

LEVEL 11: What is something that everyone has, but nobody can lose?

a woashd

_____

LEVEL 12: What has one eye that is always open? *a lednede*

_____

LEVEL 13: If you feed it, it lives. But if you water it, it dies. What is it? *erif*

_____

YOU REACHED LEVEL 13! GREAT JOB! NOW GO GET THOSE NiNJA!

PAGES 68-69:

JANNI! TEG CKBA OT
NINJA! GET BACK TO

HET OATRMNSEY WON!
THE MONASTERY NOW!

OYU NEDE OT CANEL
YOU NEED TO CLEAN

OUYR OOMRS!
YOUR ROOMS!

TI SKOOL IKLE A
IT LOOKS LIKE A

OORNTDA TIH MEHT!
TORNADO HIT THEM!

PAGES 80-81:

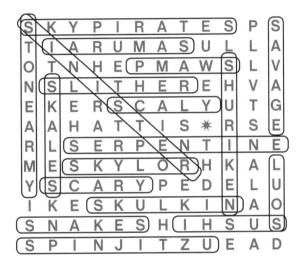

PULL THE LEVER THAT
IS SHAPED LIKE A
SNAKE'S HEAD.

PAGES 82-83:

WHY ARE CATS SO GOOD AT VIDEO GAMES?
BECAUSE THEY HAVE NINE LIVES!

PAGES 84-85:

1. **C**; 2. **D**; 3. **B**; 4. **A**

PAGES 86-87:

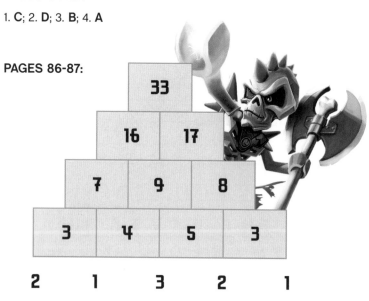

		33		
	16		17	
7		9		8
3	4		5	3

2   1   3   2   1

PAGES 88-89:

1. **MOST** 2. **GOLD** 3. **REST** 4. **HEAT**

PAGES 90-91:

1. **A CLOCK**
2. **AN EGG**
3, **YOUR AGE**
4. **TEAPOT**
5. **A TOWEL**
6. **YESTERDAY**
7. **HEAVY METAL**
8. **TROUBLE**
9. **A SPONGE**
10. **A HOLE**
11. **A SHADOW**
12. **A NEEDLE**
13. **FIRE**